Multiplied
by
Love

Multiplied by Love

IRENE BURK HARRELL

ABINGDON
Nashville

MULTIPLIED BY LOVE

Copyright © 1976 by Abingdon

All rights in this book are reserved.

Library of Congress Cataloging in Publication Data

Harrell, Irene Burk.
  Multiplied by love.
  1. Christian life—1960— I. Title.
BV4501.2.H358   248'.4   76-15370

ISBN 0-687-27303-X

MANUFACTURED BY THE PARTHENON PRESS AT
NASHVILLE, TENNESSEE, UNITED STATES OF AMERICA

to 'Guerite

*and to the memory
of Colerain Granddaddy*

Preface

"If you love me, you will keep my commandments," Jesus said (John 14:15 RSV).

But how can I keep the commandments? How can I live the Christian life? How can I walk in the Spirit?

Have you ever asked yourself these questions, perhaps from the depths of a mood of dark discouragement, awareness of abject failure?

Well, cheer up. The answer is simple. You *can't* live the Christian life. You *can't* keep the commandments. You *can't* walk in the Spirit. And neither can I. Our best efforts at righteousness will never produce anything but filthy rags in the sight of God. It is futile for us to knock ourselves out trying to attain to any kind of perfection on our own.

We can read all the rules in the Bible, recognize their excellence, recommend and even applaud them without being one centimeter closer to what we ought to be. Paul saw that the law was good, he wanted to obey it, but, he said, "I do not act as I desire to act; on the contrary, I do what I detest. . . . I cannot be good as I desire to be, and I do wrong against my wishes. . . . (. . . Left to myself, I serve the law of God with my mind, but with my flesh I

7

serve the law of sin.) Miserable wretch that I am! Who will rescue me from this body of death?'' (Rom. 7:15,19,24,25 Moffatt).

We know we are supposed to be doers of the word, not hearers only (James 1:22). But, like Paul, we find ourselves hearing the word and doing just the opposite. Obeying the commandments cannot be accomplished through a determined by-our-own-bootstraps kind of thing where we look at the scripture, see what is required, and then set out to be righteous or die trying. That kind of effort always results in condemnation and death because there is no way we can keep the law.

The law was given to show us our sin, not to enable us to make ourselves perfect. ''If it had not been for the law,'' Paul wrote to the Romans, ''I should not have recognized sin or have known its meaning'' (Rom. 7:7 Amplified). As the law convicts us in our hearts and gives us a guilty conscience, we cry out, ''O Lord, I'm a sinner. I'm sorry I've transgressed against your law. Is there any hope for me?''

We have all known Paul's despair. Left to ourselves and our own self-improvement schemes, we get steadily worse. And when we reach the bottom of things by our own efforts, then we discover, as Paul did, that we are *not* left to ourselves! God hears our prayers and accepts the sacrifice of a broken and contrite heart. As we confess our sins, He is faithful and just to forgive us and to cleanse us from all unrighteousness—''from . . . everything not in conformity to His will in purpose, thought and action'' (I John 1:9 Amplified).

Then we can identify with Paul's cry of victory: ''I thank

God there *is* a way out through Jesus Christ our Lord. The truth is that no condemnation now hangs over the head of those who are 'in' Christ Jesus. For the new spiritual principle of life 'in' Christ Jesus lifts me out of the old vicious circle of sin and death'' (Rom. 7:25–8:2 Phillips).

Where the Spirit of the Lord is, Paul wrote to the Corinthians, ''there is freedom from trying to be saved by keeping the laws of God'' (II Cor. 3:17 TLB). Our salvation, then, is all by God's grace, not by man's efforts, ''lest any man should boast'' (Eph. 2:9 Amplified). We are not the result of our own handiwork but of His (Eph. 2:10). And we are actually changed from one degree of glory to another! ''This is the work of the Lord who is Spirit'' (II Cor. 3:18 JB).

And so, ultimately, the negative ''You can't live the Christian life'' is really good news. *We can't* live it, but *Jesus can* and will live it through us if we will let Him. He will take our old creaturehood and replace it with a new creation when we stop insisting on our do-it-myself failures and invite Him to take over and become Lord of our lives. The fruit of the Spirit that we have tried so hard and so fruitlessly to cultivate in ourselves will automatically show forth when we become vessels to hold His treasure. And we won't have to try harder. We won't have to try at all.

''If you love me,'' Jesus says, ''you will keep my commandments'' (John 14:15 RSV). Many of us have read that verse wrong all these years.

''Oh, Jesus,'' we have cried out to Him, ''we *do* love you, and we will try hard to keep the commandments.'' We *have* tried. We have tried our hearts out. But Jesus didn't tell us to *try* to keep the commandments. He said, ''You *will*

9

keep them." But we will not keep them by our own efforts. He will keep them for us, in our stead. This is at the heart of the gospel.

It was exactly because no man could keep the commandments that Jesus had to come and die for us. A new covenant had to be instituted to restore us to right relationship with God, a covenant in which nothing would be required of us but that we accept what He has already done for us.

When people came to Jesus and asked Him what work God wanted them to do, He didn't hand them a mimeographed list of rules for do-it-yourself perfection. He said plainly, "This is the work God wants you to do: believe in the one he sent" (John 6:29 TEV). The *Amplified New Testament* explains *believe* to mean "give yourself up to Him, take yourself out of your own keeping and entrust yourself into His keeping" (Acts 16:31).

When we believe that way, we are not living the Christian life, but Jesus is living it for us, in us, and through us. Not that I live, Paul wrote, but Christ lives in me (Gal. 2:20).

Our yieldedness is the only thing we can remotely call *our* part. And yet our yieldedness is also His gift to us. We cannot even say "Jesus is Lord" unless we are guided by the Holy Spirit (I Cor. 12:3). And as we are yielded, He can do the work in us.

The Christian life is not a matter of learning rules and abiding by them. It is a matter of abiding in Jesus and letting His word abide in us that He might do what He wants with us and through us. Christian living is not legalism, it is living with a living Lord.

Paul wrote to the Ephesians, "I pray that God will give

you the Spirit who will open your eyes and reveal God to you, so that you will know him'' (Eph. 1:16-17 TEV). That is exactly what the Spirit has done for me. The day I gave up running my own life and invited Him to take over, He opened my eyes and revealed Himself overwhelmingly in His written word and in all His creation. There is nowhere His voice is not heard.

In Acts 17:26-27, Paul explains to the Athenians, and to us, that God made men to live over the whole earth, fixing beforehand ''the exact times and the limits of the places where they would live. He did this so that they would look for him, and perhaps find him as they felt around for him. Yet God is actually not far from any one of us'' (TEV).

This has been true for me. How much I have learned since the Spirit came into my life in a real and recognizable way. In this and some other little books I have been led to recount some of the things I have learned. Doing so, I have thought again and again of what Jesus told Peter. ''When you have turned again, strengthen your brethren'' (Luke 22:32 RSV). When one of us turns from a wrong way back to His way, we also strengthen our brothers. That is why I share some of the steps of my walk with you and welcome your sharing with me. I praise God that when we cannot fellowship with one another face to face, we can have communion through the printed page.

''Follow me,'' Jesus tells us all, ''I am the way.'' We agree that He is the way and we mean to follow but, for all our good intentions, we find ourselves headed in wrong directions time after time. When much-needed correction comes straight at us through the lips of a mother, sister, husband, brother, preacher, friend, we are apt to make

11

excuses for ourselves, harden our hearts, refuse the counsel, and go faster down the road that leads to destruction. But when we observe a fellow pilgrim being corrected by the Holy Spirit, sometimes we are caught unawares, with our defenses down instead of bristling, our hearts soft instead of concreted, and we cry, "O Lord, forgive me. I'm just like that. I've been going the wrong way too." Humbled, as David was when Nathan told him about a little lamb, we can be turned around and can receive the blessing of His correction.

Our growth in God is never by our own efforts but always by His grace. Our part is to trust Him, and we are learning to do that. It is becoming a common thing for us to try no longer to defend ourselves when we are caught short but to confess our sin, to ask for His forgiveness, to thank Him for it, and to ask Him to set us straight again. He is always faithful to do it as we rely on Him, and we are being progressively set free to do the work He requires of us, to trust in Him. And when we are trusting Him, there is no limit to what He can do through us. The more we learn, the more we call upon Him. The more we call upon Him, the closer union we have with Him.

"If you love me, you *will* keep my commandments." Glory be to God, it's true! He has written His law on our hearts, just as He promised, and He is enabling us to will and to do His good pleasure. "If you love me— " We love Him because He first loved us, and the same love that sent Jesus to die for us sent the Spirit to live in us to keep the commandments, making the Christian life a here-and-now reality, "on earth as it is in heaven."

Contents

Multiplied by Love

Contents

Know That Nothing Can Separate You from God's Love

Last December 17, I was in a high gear of praise as I drove down a superhighway outside Raleigh, North Carolina. (Some time ago, I had learned to pray as I drove, beginning always by asking God to protect me on the highway and then going on to whatever other things I had on my prayer agenda. Sometimes I prayed for other people, sometimes for needs in my own life; sometimes I prayed in the Spirit, in a language I had never learned, without knowing what meaning the words had as I poured them forth to a listening God. At times, the praying in the Spirit would turn into singing in the Spirit, the Lord supplying the melody as well as the words. By the time I reached my destination, I always knew that I had been in the presence of the Lord. It was always good to know.)

That day, such knowledge was going to be imparted to me through a set of circumstances I had never faced before.

Suddenly, from out of nowhere, the broad side of a vanlike vehicle appeared across the highway directly in front of me. I hit the brakes, heard the squeal of tires, felt the impact of force upon force, heard the crash. Then I heard silence, felt stillness.

In the midst of the silence, I became aware of a voice. It was my own, continuing in prayer, saying, "Thank you, Jesus. Praise you, Lord."

Oh, Lord, what blessing it was to have you so palpably, overwhelmingly with me that day! How I praise you for your peace that truly passes all understanding. As I heard myself praising you, feeling blood dripping down, I was aware that my eyes were closed, and I didn't know if I was alive or dead. But really, it didn't matter one way or the other because I was with you, in heaven or on earth. Compared to that certainty, nothing else was of any great consequence.

What a marvel to me, Jesus, that my heavy station wagon was demolished but that you enabled me to walk away from it. What a marvel to me, Lord, your closeness the rest of that day and in the days that followed. How preciously present you were to us all.

Lord, I have missed that station wagon; I was sorry to have black eyes and a broken nose for Christmas and for our son's December wedding; I've stewed about the fact that I can't breathe out of my nose just right and that my face isn't quite as good as new.

But, Lord, you know it was well worth all it cost to know you that close to me, to have such unforgettable *proof* that nothing can separate your loving presence from me.

Thank you, Lord, that you filled me so full of your spirit that day. Please keep on doing that, Lord, whatever it takes.

Know That Nothing Can Separate You from God's Love

Who shall separate us from the love of Christ? shall tribulation, or distress, or persecution, or famine, or nakedness, or peril, or sword? . . . Nay, in all these things we are more than conquerors through him that loved us. For I am persuaded, that neither death, nor life, nor angels, nor principalities, nor powers, nor things present, nor things to come, Nor height, nor depth, nor any other creature, shall be able to separate us from the love of God, which is in Christ Jesus our Lord.

—Romans 8:35, 37-39

Slow Down and Get On with It

Early one morning, my brother-in-law drove to the hospital where his elderly father was to have surgery that day. Arriving at the hospital's front door before it was opened, he stood waiting until a young nursing student came along, wearing a crisply starched uniform. Learning from him that the door was locked, she took a quick glance at her wristwatch and said, "Well, there's a door on the lower level that's always open. Come along, I'll show you where it is. We can get in there."

As they hurried along together, he told her the reason for his arrival at such an early hour. "I want to see my dad before they wheel him off for surgery," he explained.

"How old is your father?" the student asked.

"He'll be eighty-two his next birthday."

The student who had been in such a rush stopped dead in her tracks. "Eighty-two!" she exclaimed. "How on earth did he ever live to be that old?" She seemed truly amazed—as if she wondered whether she herself would make it to twenty-five at the rate she was going.

Lord, the student nurse is typical of most of us. We just plain go too fast, mostly nowhere, if the truth were told.

Slow Down and Get On with It

Small wonder some think that half a century will burn them out. They'll have exceeded their total mileage expectation long before then.

O Lord, please slow us down. Show us what matters. Let unessentials be forgotten with a clear conscience.

Thanks, Lord. We've asked, feeling it's almost dangerous to do so but knowing that you can make us ready for the consequences of our rashest prayers. Hallelujah, Lord. Now let us be bolder still.

Give us your sense of priorities, Jesus. I don't remember reading that you were ever in a hurry, and yet in your thirty-three years you accomplished it all. You finished the work—everything.

Lord, make us as lovingly efficient as you are, not wasting our time on anything that isn't part of your will for us but willing to spend our whole lives in doing what pleases you and what gives glory to the Father.

Have no anxiety about anything, but in everything by prayer and supplication with thanksgiving let your requests be made known to God. And the peace of God, which passes all understanding, will keep your hearts and your minds in Christ Jesus.

—Philippians 4:6-7 RSV

Choose Life

Maria and I were shopping together. On our way into the department store where I hoped to find her a new pair of tennis shoes, we stopped to look at the outbuildings for sale, an assortment of prefabricated storage sheds for lawn mowers, bicycles, charcoal grills. Some were 7'X10', others were 10'X10'.

"Which one do you like best?" I asked her.

She thought for a moment, looked from one to the other and back again, then decided somberly, "I like the biggest one best. You'd get more fresh air."

Lord, I doubt if there'd be an ounce of fresh air in either one of those sheds set in the broiling sun. But we have a way of finding some reason, right or wrong, for liking the thing we prefer. I guess it really doesn't matter what size shed Maria liked—especially since we weren't in the market for either one—but it does matter greatly what she chooses in some other things. Lord, see that she always chooses you.

Here and now I call heaven and earth to witness against you that I have put life and death before you, the blessing

Choose Life

and the curse: choose life, then, that you and your children may live, by loving the Eternal your God, obeying his voice, and holding fast to him, for that means life to you and length of days.

—Deuteronomy 30:19-20 Moffatt

Deny Yourself

Dishes finally done, little people tucked in bed for the night at last, I heaved a sigh of relief as I sat down at my desk in the study. It had been a long day, and I was glad that the hardest part of it was over. It would be almost like vacation to sit at my desk for a couple of hours to finish some deadline work and then go to bed.

But I had no sooner picked up my pen than I heard the crunch of a car turning in our driveway. A woman's voice called out a greeting to my husband who was raking pine straw in the front yard. I almost groaned aloud. There was no mistaking *that* voice.

"Is Irene at home?"

"Yes, she's inside."

"Oh, no," I moaned to myself. "Not her. Please God, not tonight."

The woman was someone I knew well from having listened to her for interminable hours on the telephone during the last few years. We had prayed with her and for her and had sought the intercessions of others on her behalf a million times without seeing any permanent improvement.

She kept shying away from real commitment to a fellowship that would have been a stabilizing influence and an avenue for growth in her life.

Oh, there had been some good days when she wouldn't call at all or would telephone rationally and briefly about some specific matter. But mostly it was an ever-widening, unending circle, rehashing the same old confidentialities—"I've never told this to anyone before in my entire life"—forgetting that she'd told it so many times that you knew it by heart.

No, I wouldn't listen this time. I wouldn't stick my head out the door, plaster a fake smile on my face, and call out a lying welcome, "Come on in. It's good to see you." Maybe she would get so engrossed in talking to my husband that she'd forget all about me. At least he could go on with his raking while she talked.

Being careful to stay out of the line of vision of windows at that end of the yard, I slunk upstairs. If she came in, I could always be just getting into the bathtub or handling an urgent cry for attention from one of the little people.

I sat down to wait it out on the top step of the darkened stairway, ready to fly into appropriate diversionary action if I heard the door open. Anything would be better than having to listen to the over and over and over of her broken record again.

After a long time, the murmur of voices in the yard stopped. Then a motor started, and, looking out a darkened bedroom window, I saw the car drive off. I went back downstairs to work, though not free. I was burdened with a heavy conscience of unlove.

Multiplied by Love

Lord, this kind of thing has happened before in my life. Other people tell me it happens to them too. We put up elaborate defense mechanisms to avoid confrontations with persons who are in obvious need of our patience and love. Whether we can see that it does them any good is not the point. And however it looks and feels momentarily—the relief of having escaped this time—we are defeated by our victory.

What are we supposed to do, Lord? Always be doormats? Always be on the defensive? Or is there something we haven't taken hold of yet that would bring victory and abundant life, releasing us from this bondage of unsatisfactory relationships? Reveal it to us, Lord.

Oh, thank you, Lord, for showing us so plainly that *our* victory is always defeat. The only way to win is to do it your way, and then the victory is yours. Hallelujah!

Then Jesus said to his disciples, "If anyone wants to follow in my footsteps he must give up all right to himself, take up his cross and follow me. For the man who wants to save his life will lose it; but the man who loses his life for my sake will find it. For what good is it for a man to gain the whole world at the price of his real life?"
—Matthew 16:24-26 Phillips

Don't Be Double-Minded

Trapeze

Split-level prayers
keep us dangling
            between
confident faith
            and
desperate hope.

Will we rise
            or fall?
We cannot know
until we leap.

            But
God knows—
            and cares.

Lord, let me always leap—in your direction. Let me always be zeroed in on your wavelength, never double-minded, never split in my loyalties where you're concerned.

Multiplied by Love

Lord, today I don't have enough devotion to pray for a mind like Jesus' and a life to match, but please, Lord, head me in that direction.

But you must believe when you pray, and not doubt at all. Whoever doubts is like a wave in the sea that is driven and blown about by the wind. Such a person is a hyprocrite, undecided in all he does, and he must not think that he will receive anything from the Lord.
—James 1:6-8 TEV

A double-minded man is unstable in all his ways.
—James 1:8

Forget the Past

Calendar work plays an important part in the education of deaf and hard-of-hearing children. Our Marguerite was forever making calendars, marking off little squares and numbering them, abbreviating the names of the days of the week. If we were having a rainy day, she'd draw an umbrella, if a sunny one, a smiling-faced old Sol. She didn't call her creation a calendar at first, though. She called it her "today-tomorrow." In the beginning, she didn't talk much about yesterday, just crossed it out when the new day began. She didn't glory in yesterday's success, nor wallow in grief at its failures, but started each new "today" afresh, looking forward to the next one.

Lord, Marguerite knows about yesterdays, now, and often prefaces her remarks with "A long time ago" as she tells us something from the past. I'm glad that she has learned to do that, that she has such an excellent memory for what has gone before and such words to remind us too. How much she has learned!

But I can learn something from 'Guerite's former preoccupation with only today-tomorrow, can't I? Not to be discouraged about what I have done or failed to do in the yesterdays, nor to rest on alleged laurels, but to live in the todays and look forward to the glorious tomorrows. Thanks, Lord. Especially for your grace in forgiving all my yesterdays.

Forgetting the past and looking forward to what lies ahead, I strain to reach the end of the race and receive the prize for which God is calling us up to heaven because of what Christ Jesus did for us.
—Philippians 3:13-14 TLB

Control Your Tongue

Suddenly unexpectedly hospitalized with a trick knee that required immediate surgery, my daughter Alice needed some time to think, to talk, to tell me what I needed to do for her—whom I needed to call to get her school assignments and her books, what to bring from home, what to buy, whom to notify that she wouldn't be able to fulfill her outside commitments for a few days.

But silence for thinking and planning, for getting our heads together, was nonexistent. Alice had been assigned to a hospital room that already had a patient in it. The other woman couldn't stop talking. She kept describing the size of her hernia: "It won't [*sic*] hardly as big as the last joint of my little finger"; the pain of the shot prior to surgery: "It stung like hot pepper in that needle"; the agonies of bedpans: "I thought it would near about run over the first time I could wet in it"; the volume of postoperative abdominal gas pressure in her: "If you hear something like a bomb go off in the middle of the night, don't worry. It'll just be me." She laughed, then more seriously added, "I'm glad that so far there hain't been any odor to it," and so on *ad infinitum*.

Next, we heard all about the adventures and misadventures of all her relatives and her relatives' kinfolk. She knew—and named—everybody's age. Then there was a recent front-page husband/wife murder-suicide—'They lived right under me, not half a mile from the house''—about which she divulged fascinating details not mentioned in the newspaper account.

Well, it wasn't easy, but Alice and I got our thinking done, our plans made in the midst of it. We just had to put our minds out of gear as far as receiving foreign input was concerned. And the woman didn't seem to mind our inattention to her. Her own ears were appreciative of all she had to say, and that was the only listening audience she really needed. When the flow finally stopped for a minute, I was careful to let the silence hang silent, not to make any comments just to be polite or ask any questions that would start the barrage flowing again.

Lord, that woman was cheerful in the midst of all that had gone wrong in her case. And I know that counts for something. I'm glad you gave my daughter such a cheery roommate, one so friendly, so willing to share her life, instead of some miserable crosspatch grumping to herself.

But, Lord, let me learn from her too-much talking that there are times when I should be quiet and let people think about their own affairs.

I tell you this: on the Judgment Day everyone will have to give account of every useless word he has ever spoken.

—Matthew 12:36 TEV

Ask for Wisdom

I was flying in a big jet with my ten-year-old. She was sitting beside the window, watching everything with great interest as we approached Washington National Airport for a landing. Suddenly, the pilot banked the plane for his turn, and her window framed a dull stretch of open sky. The ground was out of sight. 'Guerite voiced a small protest and bounced up and down in her seat a couple of times, trying to tip the plane back the way it had been. Almost simultaneously, the plane turned back to level flight, the Pentagon appeared full in her vision below, and she was satisfied that her efforts had been rewarded.

Lord, you and I know that Marguerite's bouncing had nothing to do with that plane's angle and direction. Her childlike naïveté makes me wonder how often my efforts are that futile, how often they have nothing whatsoever to do with how things turn out, because the forces in motion are so great that no effort of mine could make a difference.

Lord, give me your wisdom in this. Show me, day by day, when and to what purpose my action is required. Lord, give me strength and wisdom to act—and strength and wisdom not to act—according to your eternal purpose. And let all in me that has been futile and useless be made fruitful and useful to you.

If you want to know what God wants you to do, ask him, and he will gladly tell you, for he is always ready to give a bountiful supply of wisdom to all who ask him.
—James 1:5 TLB

Reflect My Glory

Driving through the morning fog, I couldn't see the sun. But the yellow maples could. And they reflected the sun's glory back at him and out at me.

Lord, I'd like it to be that, even when I can't see you, I'd be like the maples and show you to others because I have such a certainty you're there. Thank you, Lord, that you give us that inner certainty even when we're temporarily blinded to the outward evidence of you.

Let your light so shine before men, that they may see your good works, and glorify your Father which is in heaven.

—Matthew 5:16

Don't Despair

I've never been a prize athlete. But when I was in about the seventh grade, I used to play softball with the other girls at school. I didn't have much to do in a game. Three strikes and I was out, more times than not, and the outfield position where they put me in the off innings was safely beyond the batting range of most of the girls.

The ball game was definitely dull for me. Pitchers and catchers were the only ones who always got to do something, I observed. Instinctively knowing I could never make it as a catcher, I kept yearning for the day when a miracle would happen and I'd be allowed to pitch.

Unbelievably, such a day arrived in the late spring. Our beloved Coach Pemberton, a blond, curly-haired young man—all the girls were not-so-secretly in love with him—decided I could occupy the pitcher's mound.

I was in seventh heaven, but not for long. On my way out to the mound I was confronted with the sickening revelation that the elastic in the top of my peach-colored rayon panties was losing its grip. With every step, I felt them inching precariously lower and lower on my hips.

Eventually, I reached the mound, but every pitch was an agony of suspense. I was shamefully conscious of the coach's standing directly behind me as I tried to throw the ball while keeping my legs tight together, my elbows ground into my hips to keep my unmentionables from slithering below my skirt to the dust where they would be seen and mentioned by everybody.

Several of my pitches *rolled* across home plate. Some of them never reached it.

I walked four batters in a row before I was delivered. Speechless, the coach shook his head in incredulity and nodded, mercifully, toward the bench. I headed for it, hobbling with an interminable number of tiny stilt-legged steps, and settled down onto the weathered gray seat as inconspicuously as possible. There, I pretended intense preoccupation with the game while I worked feverishly to rescue myself from a disgrace I'd never live down.

By a combination of stealthily sliding forward on the bench a few times and giving my about-to-leave-me step-ins a couple of hearty tugs behind my back, I maneuvered them into a position high enough to enable me to escape to the girl's restroom. Dashing into a booth, I unlocked my legs, let gravity take over, wrapped the hateful garment in a couple of paper towels, buried them in the bottom of the trash can, and went back to class for business as usual.

I was never asked to pitch again. Somehow I never wanted to.

O Lord, how I laughed, remembering this that was at the time so painfully humiliating that I could have cried about it. Growing up is full of things like that. Years later, the

37

remembering is priceless; we wouldn't have had it *not* happen for anything.

It seems it would be good for me to keep that in mind when difficult things happen to me today, things that are a part of my still growing up. Somehow, I sense you will redeem every experience—even the most painful—and use it for good if I trust you. Thank you, Lord, for reminding me of that. Help me apply that confidence to the things I'm going through today.

In my opinion whatever we may have to go through now is less than nothing compared with the magnificent future God has in store for us.

—Romans 8:18 Phillips

Don't Be Conformed to This World

Hide and Seek

Sometimes,
All-of-a-sudden,
Death says
"Ready or not,
Here I come!"
And does,
To one we know.

Was she ready?
Will I be?
Not usually.
We're too busy
Living or dying
To get ready
For death.

But that doesn't
Make him wait.
He finds us

Multiplied by Love

> Where we are
> And never cries
> "All that's out
> May come in free!"

Lord, that's how it was when I was conformed to the world. I saw people die, unready, and I was broken with grief. That's how I'd have died then, too—unready and broken. I wouldn't have known the first thing about how to get ready.

Lord, I thank you that it's different for me now. You have prepared me abundantly for everything you have permitted to happen in my life. And I know I can trust you to have me ready for dying too.

Oh, how rich I am to know you, Lord, to be able to trust you with everything. Let my life shine forth with that confidence wherever I go.

Sanctify the Lord God in your hearts: and be ready always to give an answer to every man that asketh you a reason of the hope that is in you.

—I Peter 3:15

Come as a Child

Nothing unusual about the telephone's ringing; it does that all the time at our house. But the voice that said ''Is this Judge Harrell's residence?'' was that of a child.

After my ''Yes, it is. May I help you?'' the small voice said rather breathlessly, expecting a no, ''Does he take home calls?''

''Yes.''

''From children?'' There was rising incredulity in her voice.

''Oh, yes.''

We set up a time for her to call back, a time when the judge would be at home.

Lord, I loved that whole conversation: the politeness of the child; her thinking that maybe a child would be beneath the judge's notice, not knowing that he has always paid more attention to children than to grown-ups; the joy in her.

Lord, I don't know whether she called back or not. I haven't any idea what she wanted, but, Lord, if that child's joy at the hope of being received has anything to do with

41

what heaven will be about, I want to be in on it. Let me come as a child, expecting almost nothing, receiving it all.

Jesus said, "Let the little children come to me, and do not hinder them, for the kingdom of heaven belongs to such as these."

—*Matthew 19:14 NIV*

If There Be
Anything Lovely,
Think About It

Shopping with one of my beautiful daughters the other day, I noticed a spectacularly broad-hipped woman going into the dressing room to try on a two-piece outfit. A few minutes later she emerged, looking rather crestfallen, and hung the garment on a rack by the cash-register desk.

"How was it? Did it fit?" the clerk asked her routinely.

"Yeah, it fit. But it didn't look good. Those little tops just don't hang down over great big bottoms the way they ought to."

With that, she tugged at the jacket of her old outfit and waddled away, the jacket riding up with every step until it rested wrinkled and at home on the shelf of her bulging derriere.

Lord, lots of times I blame the manufacturers for cutting things too skimpily instead of blaming myself for eating too abundantly, exercising too seldom. I could solve it simply by admitting that I really wear a size larger than I'm willing to buy, but that wouldn't help. Soon I'd expand to fill the larger size overfull, and I'd be even worse off than before.

In the old days, women didn't wear such form-revealing

things. Their girth could remain a softly comfortable secret under flowing robes. I'm always thinking I'd like that for now, especially because sometimes my too-plumpness subtracts free-flowing joy from me, makes me look at myself so disapprovingly that I can't smile at anyone— thick or thin.

Lord, as I look around me I see people of all sizes and shapes. And I don't see you condemning anyone for not measuring up to fashion-plate figures. As a matter of fact, you act as if you made us in all sizes and shapes on purpose.

Lord, show us your truth in this. Give each of us to conform to the standard you have planned for us, whatever that is. And meeting that standard, let us be so accepting of ourselves that we won't need to think of *us* anymore but will be set free to be *your* witnesses, to see what you're doing, and do likewise.

Fix your thoughts on what is true and good and right. Think about things that are pure and lovely, and dwell on the fine, good things in others. Think about all you can praise God for and be glad about.
—Philippians 4:8 TLB

May the God of peace himself make you entirely pure and devoted to God; and may your spirit and soul and body be kept strong and blameless until that day when our Lord Jesus Christ comes back again. God, who called you to become his child, will do all this for you, just as he promised.
—I Thessalonians 5:23-24 TLB

Receive the Kingdom

Our hard-of-hearing daughter was nine years old and ready to preach her first sermon. She seated her family and a few guests on the brick steps at the back of the house, then climbed up into the nearby treehouse from which she would deliver her profundities. We were ready to listen as she began in solemn tones to give us the word for the day:

"God looks everywhere" (delivered slowly and majestically, her eyes searching us all). "Do not bite people; do not pinch people; do not kick people" (a little thud reverberating from the treehouse indicated she was giving a demonstration where we couldn't see it). "Do not bother people" (she wrenched at her shoulder), "because it hurts. They have a sunburn."

After these directions for a good life, she pretended to prepare a communion, pouring her imagination into an assortment of Mickey Mouse cups, downed every portion herself, and then keeled over on her back, out of sight, obviously "slain in the Spirit." A few moments later, she emerged through the trap door, climbed down the little ladder, walked among her congregation, and laid hands on each one's head in turn, proclaiming some kind of blessing on us all.

We had been to church.

Multiplied by Love

Thank you, Lord, for the times when you let little children lead us. And thanks, Lord, that you lead them yourself.

And when the chief priests and scribes saw the wonderful things that he did, and the children crying in the temple, and saying, Hosanna to the son of David; they were sore displeased. And said unto him, Hearest thou what these say? And Jesus saith unto them, Yea; have ye never read, Out of the mouth of babes and sucklings thou hast perfected praise?

—Matthew 21:15-16

Verily I say unto you, Whosoever shall not receive the kingdom of God as a little child shall in no wise enter therein.

—Luke 18:17

Feed on My Word

A friend of ours remarked one day that he was never hungry. I wondered why. He looked well-nourished, husky, robust, vigorous, though not fat. Knowing the menfolk in my tribe, I found it hard to believe there was a strong healthy man who was never hungry.

When we spent a weekend with him at a meeting, I found out why.

Before supper he had a soft drink. At the restaurant he asked the waitress for extra coffee before she brought our food, and he almost single-handedly emptied the tray of crackers which was on the table.

The next day after breakfast he opened a couple of packs of chewing gum and shared them with the rest of us. During the morning meeting, he was consuming candy mints by the roll.

Our friend is never hungry—because he doesn't give himself a chance to be. He makes constant provision for being fed all the time. Hunger doesn't have a chance to get a foothold in such a man.

Lord, I know that's how we all need to be about your Word—feeding so constantly, so continually that our hunger is always being assuaged. Lord, make me live according to what I know.

> *How blessed is the man who does not walk in the counsel of the wicked, Nor stand in the path of sinners, Nor sit in the seat of scoffers! But his delight is in the law of the Lord, And in His law he meditates day and night. And he will be like a tree firmly planted by streams of water, Which yields its fruit in its season, And its leaf does not wither; And in whatever he does, he prospers.*
> —*Psalm 1:1-3 NAS*

Get Ready for Whatever

Sitting in a chair a few feet from the foot of my father-in-law's hospital bed, I was aware of the small lump his wasted body made beneath the too-white sheets. I had sat with him off and on for two days. His mouth was usually agape, his parched lips motionless in sleep, his eyes closed unless he was awake and we were talking about something. But in the afternoon of the second day, I began to notice something else. The lips frequently stirred, methodically, in various earnest configurations, the eyelids were fluttery, open and closed, but the face alert.

There were occasional audible uh-huhs of agreement when his lips had been silent for a while, and I knew the conversation wasn't one-sided dream talking, but real two-way talk. When his lips were still, he was listening to somebody. Somehow I knew not to interrupt.

Later, when I needed to give him a drink of water, I asked about it.

"Granddaddy, did you know you've been lying here moving your mouth as if you were talking to somebody—only I couldn't understand you because no sound was coming out?"

He looked at me and grinned sheepishly. "Yessum," he said. "I knowed it."

49

He didn't volunteer anything more, and I didn't ask. But when he had finished the water and I had sat back down, he blurted out, "I was just a lyin' here wonderin' where we're all gonna go."

"To heaven, Granddaddy, we're all going to go to heaven," my daughter who had come to visit asserted.

"Yes," I added, "because we're trusting Jesus to get us there."

Granddaddy wanted me to tell him the Ten Commandments then, and I turned to Exodus 20 in the Bible on my lap and read them to him. We talked about the Golden Rule and how Jesus had summed up for us all the law and the prophets into two commandments—love God with all your heart, soul, and mind; love your neighbor as yourself.

Granddaddy nodded, then resumed his silent conversation with the Lord.

Lord, I'm so thankful that you gave me an opportunity to be with Granddaddy as he was making his preparations to slip away from earth and be with you. It was such a sweet time for love to grow, not in one fell swoop but gradually, to bursting fullness, as sons and sisters and grandchildren and in-laws and nieces came to visit and to love him.

And I thank you for showing to me, who usually talks too much, that I needed to provide for loving silence with my companionship so that the sick one might hear your voice.

And I heard a voice from heaven saying unto me, Write, Blessed are the dead which die in the Lord from henceforth: Yea, saith the Spirit, that they may rest from their labours.

—Revelation 14:13

Dwell in Unity

A teen exceedingly precious to me was having some difficulties in her relationship with her youngest sister. After overhearing one particularly unpleasant encounter between them, I spoke to the older girl about it.

"Aren't you being a little bit artificial when you talk to your little sister?" I ventured. "You've been so cross with her today. And even when you say friendly things, you put on a false voice or something—you sound fakey."

"Well," she barked the challenge at me, "which would you rather I do, be fake or knock her block off?"

Just like me, Lord, just like me. The alternatives I give myself to choose from are often that limited and limiting. I set up for myself and choose from alternatives, none of which is good or desirable. Help me, Lord, and help that child to see that the choice *you* give us—in all things—is not between evil and worse evil, but between evil and good. That choosing the good will often involve our dying to self doesn't mean there will be less blessing in it for us, but greater blessing because we have chosen your way of love, we have permitted our hindering selves to die a little more.

Multiplied by Love

Thanks, Lord. And do help these two to love each other in a real way, your way.

Behold, how good and how pleasant it is for brethren to dwell together in unity!

—*Psalm 133:1*

Obey the Law

One of the best friends I'll ever have is a woman named Virginia. Her upbringing was very different from mine. When she was only nine years old—and tiny for her age—she was working in the tobacco fields in eastern North Carolina. One day her employer decided that she should be the one to drive the hired hands home at the end of their day's work. He piled cushions and newspapers on the car seat so Virginia would be able to see out, taught her the rudiments of the gears, and told her to be on her way. The men she was driving would be able to tell her where they lived, and she could find her own way back home, asking for directions if she lost her way.

When Virginia protested that she couldn't drive on the highway because she had no driver's license, her boss brushed the objection aside. ''Aw, you don't need no license 'til you get caught.''

Lord, how many things in life we handle in that fashion. We do, or encourage others to do, things that are contrary to the law of God, and if they protest or if our inner selves cringe, we say, "Aw, it'll be all right—but don't get caught."

What this kind of permissiveness has done to our souls, I shiver to contemplate. Giving them an inch, we've opened barn doors wide for the devil and all his cohorts to march in and take over. Forgive us, Lord, and let us go the right way from now on, obeying the law of the land—and your law—in everything.

For the Lord's sake, obey every law of your government: those of the king as head of the state, and those of the king's officers, for he has sent them to punish all who do wrong, and to honor those who do right. . . . You are free from the law, but that doesn't mean you are free to do wrong. Live as those who are free to do only God's will at all times.

—I Peter 2:13-14, 16 TLB

Acknowledge God

Tommy

My winter-surfing son
   wet suited
   brown bearded
   red with wind
   shivering
   waiting for the wave
     wiping out
Beautiful.

Lord, it would take ten strong men to throw me in that icy roaring water. It's funny how kids can be so lazy when they're asked to work, so complaining when they're asked to do something outside if it's sprinkling even a little bit. But give them a chance to go surfing, and they'll drive a million miles, brave below-freezing gales just for the chance to ride a wave.

I've asked them about it and am beginning to understand just a little bit. The reason they like surfing so much is really because you're the one who's in charge out there on the ocean, and that's exciting and wonderful to them.

Multiplied by Love

Lord, it pleases me to know that. Somehow, get our surfing sons to let you take that kind of command of the dry-land part of their lives too. Show them the wonderfulness of acknowledging that you're in control of it all, all the time. (And plant that knowledge so firmly in *my* mind that I won't forget for an instant.)

It is good to say, "Thank you" to the Lord, to sing praises to the God who is above all gods. Every morning tell him, "Thank you for your kindness," and every evening rejoice in all his faithfulness. Sing his praises. . . . You have done so much for me, O Lord. No wonder I am glad! I sing for joy.

—Psalm 92:1-4 TLB

O Lord, you have reigned from prehistoric times, from the everlasting past. The mighty oceans thunder your praise. You are mightier than all the breakers pounding on the seashores of the world!

—Psalm 93:2-4 TLB

Look on Your Heart

The four of us had been out in a small boat all day, fishing for fish that weren't interested in our bait. There was my husband, his friend, the friend's wife, and I. We all got hungry and thirsty and sunburned and tired before we finally headed for the shore.

Our host's wife looked awful, I thought. She was getting so burned, her face a painful red. We were as windblown a crew as you've ever seen when we pulled up to the dock and raced for the restrooms.

I got the shock of my life when I stopped in front of the mirror on my way out. I had thought our host's wife looked bad, but I looked much worse. What must she have thought about me? My hair was sun dried, bristling out dully in every direction, my face red past remedying, the total effect more Halloween than real.

I washed my face, tried to brush my hair down, and put on my dark glasses again. There wasn't much sun left outside to worry about, but the glasses would help to hide my face from others and even from myself when I looked back in the mirror.

Multiplied by Love

Lord, it's a funny thing about sunglasses. They make us look better to ourselves because we see less well through them. And when we look better to ourselves, we probably act better toward other people. But really, why should the awareness that we look less than lovely make us act more unlovely than usual? It shouldn't, I know, but it seems to, not just in my case, but in the case of people I know.

One day one of our teen-agers came home from school in a snarly mood. She had been out of sorts for several days, and I had let it pass, praying for her, but not saying anything to her about her general ugliness toward people.

After overhearing a particularly unpleasant confrontation between her and a younger child, I decided to get at the root of it.

I began in as loving a tone as I could muster. "Is something bothering you lately? You seem kind of unhappy—"

"I'm too fat," she wailed and started to cry.

"What do you weigh?" I prodded sympathetically, thinking she was as near the right size and shape as anyone could be.

"A hundred and thirty—and that's what *you* were going to try to get down to!"

That a teen-age daughter would weigh the same as her plumpish mother's goal (always out of reach by a good ten or fifteen pounds) was just too much for her. Outwardly, I resolved to help the situation by planning meals a little more carefully, cooking less-fattening things, and inwardly I rejoiced that I had a good excuse to stay on the round side—so my daughter would not feel inferior.

Look on Your Heart

Lord, it's important, isn't it, to accept ourselves exactly as we are because when we don't, we're likely to take our uncomfortableness about ourselves out on other people, making them uncomfortable, too, in a whole vicious circle of unacceptance.

I know some beautiful—in you, Lord—thin people. I know some beautiful—in you, Lord—round people. And I can't see that you prefer one above the other, but you love both kinds infinitely. I'm tired of all the unrealistic views of what a perfect specimen would be. I'm ready to stop looking at the size of my exterior and start examining my heart. Do I have enough capacity of heart to receive all the blessings you want to give me? And to impart them to others? If I don't, Lord, enlarge my heart. That's so important, you can forget about shrinking my outside.

The Lord said unto Samuel, Look not on his countenance, or on the height of his stature; . . . for the Lord seeth not as man seeth; for man looketh on the outward appearance, but the Lord looketh on the heart.

—I Samuel 16:7

See That It Is Good

Point of View

Multiplied by love
   the sky deepens its blue
  and grass is
    green satin.

Lord, everything looked brand-new to me after I met you. That was more than eight years ago now, and the brand-newness of a world seen through a heightened awareness of your reality hasn't diminished but grows and grows.

But, Lord, I'm afraid I'm going to have to ask you to "turn it down" just a little. There have been some days lately when I was so filled with awareness of your love that I couldn't look at the clouds without weeping at their beauty.

Lord, since I live in the midst of the world, don't you think that's a little bit too much? After all, they were just rain clouds, a kind of dingy gray.

Since earliest times men have seen the earth and sky and all God made, and have known of his existence and great eternal power.

—Romans 1:20 TLB

Don't Be a Busybody

Two handsomely suited women—probably rich—stirred among the books on the table in front of me at an autograph party. I caught an imperfect snatch of their conversation, something about a birthday party and something about being ninety years old. Wanting to make some kind of conversation with them, I had voiced my disbelief when I said, incredulity in my every word, "You're going to be ninety?!"

It turned out they were talking about a friend for whose birthday present they were shopping. The look on their faces as they walked away (*without* buying one of my books) was, mercifully, one I can't describe. Talk about embarrassment, I felt *such* a fool!

Lord, I'm forever doing things like that—butting in, hurting someone else's feelings—when I'd be better off keeping my mouth shut. What makes me like that? And can you make me better, please? I'd still like to grow up—even though it's hard at my age.

Don't let me hear of your suffering for . . . being a busybody and prying into other people's affairs.
—I Peter 4:15 TLB

Renew Your Mind

Extremists

Some people live deeply;
Others keep neat houses.
I have two friends:

One's favorite phrase is
"When I get straightened around
I'll do thus and so."
And you know something?
She's never done anything yet—
Significant, that is.
Oh, she'll smoke a cigarette
(A habit she'll give up
When she gets straightened around)
Or spend hours reading the latest *Reader's Digest*,
Perched, uncomfortable, on the edge
Of an immaculate chair,
But she can't sit back and read a book,
She's not straightened around enough for that.

Renew Your Mind

The other can see no shambles
When the house is falling down around,
But lights romantic candles
When yesterday's garbage
Is still not carried out.
Or she'll sew a gossamer gown
With the room knee deep in dust
And never see it.
She lives, and when she dies
She'll have done most of the things she's wanted to.
And her many friends,
Who've eaten her cakes,
And been visited when they were sick,
Will clean up her house for the funeral.

Lord, you showed me this truth long ago, but I confess I'm *still* more like the first friend than the second one. Oh, I don't mean that I have an immaculate chair anywhere or that I don't read books or that I smoke cigarettes. Those particular things don't happen to apply to me, but, Lord, I don't live as deeply as I ought. There are *important* things I keep putting off, all because I let unimportant things rob me of my time. Why, just last night, I caught myself reading through some ridiculous mail-order catalog—I wasn't planning to order anything—when your Word was within reach of my easy chair. And just last week I wasted a whole sunny Sunday afternoon laboring over some ridiculous dime-store jigsaw puzzle when I could have been out visiting the sick or writing letters to faraway shut-ins.

Multiplied by Love

Forgive me, Lord, and keep on making me aware that I have chosen you and ought to live every moment of my life to the praise of your glory.

Be not conformed to this world: but be ye transformed by the renewing of your mind, that ye may prove what is that good, and acceptable, and perfect, will of God.
—Romans 12:2

Judge Not

At breakfast one morning, her brown eyes twinkling up at me, Maria delivered a solemn pronouncement: "Mama, I'm gonna be a judge."

"You are?" How pleased her daddy would be that she wanted to follow in his footsteps! He had wanted one of his kids to be a judge or to study law at least, but neither the boys nor the older girls had shown any interest in that direction. I had supposed that Maria's loving to go to court with her daddy was connected with the fact that everyone always gave her lots of candy and chewing gum there. But apparently there was a deeper interest.

"Maria, that's just wonderful," I told her, thinking how beautiful her black curls would look above a judge's robe. "Daddy will be so happy about it."

"Yeah!" our five-year-old went on, adding my enthusiasm to her own. "Laura's gonna let me be the judge in her cat show."

Well, Lord, leaping to unwarranted conclusions seems to be my specialty, doesn't it? I'm thankful that this time it didn't get me in any trouble but just provided a good laugh for us all. And, Lord, I'm really glad Maria probably *won't* grow up to be a judge—except maybe at cat shows. Judging violators of the law of the land is man's business, difficult business, sometimes ugly and dangerous business too.

Lord, I pray for judges, especially for the one who heads this family. I'm so thankful for the relationship he has with you—that makes it possible for him to receive wisdom and discernment through your Holy Spirit. He couldn't get along without it.

And when the Lord raised them up judges, then the Lord was with the judge.

—Judges 2:18

Pray Without Ceasing

When a neighborhood teen-ager came into the study where I was working one night, I didn't even look up. He was almost like a member of our own family walking in, a kid who had practically lived at our house some days, being a good friend to our boys and to our girls. His younger sister had been a best friend too, and his older sister a baby-sitter for us once upon a time. I loved the whole family—nice, quiet, decent, hard-working people.

Assuming, if I even stopped to think about it, that the boy was waiting for one of the kids to come down from upstairs or something, I kept reading galleys for a new book through the reading glasses perched on my nose. But gradually I became aware of his standing there, as if he wanted to see me, and so I looked up.

"Hi! Anything I can do for you?"

Much to my surprise, I found myself listening to a poured-out broken heart.

There was no worldly practical advice I could give him about his dilemma, so I advised him to do what I often had to do when faced with a situation my own intellect couldn't handle.

"Can't you just trust the Lord to guide you in this?" I suggested. "Just let Him lead you step by step as you live one day at a time?"

I expected at least a reluctant, "Well, I suppose so," and I knew that God could handle it even on that grudging basis. But the answer I got was a flat no.

"Really? Why not?"

The answer was that he didn't have a Lord to trust. Further conversation brought out that so far he believed that *someone* had created all that was—the trees, the ocean, the sky—but as to which god, well, one was as good as the next one as far as he could see. And it didn't much matter what a guy believed in just as long as he believed in something.

I was heartsick, witnessed bumblingly, excruciatingly aware of what a profoundly poor witness my life must have been to him day in and day out as he saw me tired or cross or unreasonable or unloving toward the children. I had never put on company manners for him or for any other neighborhood kid.

Putting my failure out of my mind I talked a little, reminding him of some of the spectacular things God had done for our family since our discovery of His reality and of some things He had done for other people we knew or had heard about.

He offered no comment, just stood there, and, after a little, he turned to go.

"Wait just a minute," I told him, holding out my hand. "Would you let me pray with you before you leave?"

No, he wouldn't care for that, he said. Religion to him

was a kind of private thing. But when I asked him to please wait a minute then while I prayed aloud by myself, he paused in the doorway. I don't know whether he closed his eyes or not, but I closed mine. I didn't pray for God to perform a right-then-and-there miracle for him (I specifically asked God *not* to do that), but I asked God to work in the boy's life and reveal His love to him, according to His perfect will.

Tears were dripping profusely from my eyes onto the top of my desk, I kept hearing his *sniff, sniff,* and then he was gone. Later that night, my daughter and I and then my husband and I claimed God's promise that if two of us agreed on earth as touching anything, it would be done for them in heaven. We agreed together that the young man would become a ''Jesus people,'' utterly committed to Him.

In the days that followed, we handed him exciting spiritual books to read and prayed for him again and again as the Holy Spirit brought the matter to our minds.

What really hit me was that here was a kid who had been in and out of our house so much that I treated him like part of the furniture, and I didn't even *know* that he wasn't a Christian. How many others might there have been over the years—people who knew of *our* faith, but people to whom we never spoke personally, inviting them to receive this Jesus for themselves?

Lord, I thank you for that boy's broken heart. Thank you that no ordinary solution would do and that you used his distress to reveal to us that he had no one to call Lord.

Father, I thank you for the way you heard and answered our prayers for him above all we could ask or think, that today Jimmy is one of the most thoroughly "lit" Christian boys we know—and that others have come to believe because of him.

Pray without ceasing.

—I Thessalonians 5:17

Know That I Am
with You Always

Last summer, my husband's father graduated to glory. Marguerite, our ten-year-old with two hearing aids, saw what it was all about in the perfect way that only one who hears God can see it.

We were at the home of one of my husband's brothers. The little white frame church where the funeral service was to be held was just across the street. Before time for the service, many people were going in and out to "see Granddaddy." I saw Marguerite watching them and considered whether I should let her go. As it turned out, it wasn't my decision.

"Is Granddaddy over there?" she asked me.

I gave her a qualified yes.

"I want to see Granddaddy," she said, matter of factly.

I took her hand, and we walked across the street and up the stairs into the cool sanctuary. Marguerite went close to the open casket, looked long and seriously without saying anything, and then turned to go. As we walked back down the aisle, she put her right hand on her left arm and began to feel all up and down it, a puzzled expression on her face. I wondered what she was thinking.

Turning her eyes up to me so she could see what I would say to her, she asked, "No bones?"

I explained in words she already knew that Granddaddy's bones were still in place, but that the part of him that talked to her and tickled her and let her sit on his lap was not inside him anymore.

"That part of Granddaddy is called his spirit," I said. "Granddaddy's spirit is not in his body anymore. His spirit has gone to heaven."

"Oh. With Jesus," she said, perfectly contented. I nodded my head, and her questions ended. Marguerite was more than satisfied. And so was I.

Lord, I'm so thankful that you give such perfect understanding to your little ones. Thank you, Lord, that you have put such a little one in the midst of our family. Thank you for showing 'Guerite that something had left Granddaddy—and especially for giving her the faith to know that *that* something is not lost but is with you.

And Jesus prayed this prayer: "O Father, Lord of heaven and earth, thank you for hiding the truth from those who think themselves so wise, and for revealing it to little children."

—Matthew 11:25 TLB

Drink of Living Water

Drought

The world breathes dust:
An acrid pall of woodsmoke
   wreathes the forest;
Grass crunches under foot
   past remembering water;
Dogwood leaves hang limp
   panting their thirst for rain.
A breeze begins
   stirring up clouds
     of parched earth
   sending down sharp-needled showers
     of brittle pine straw—

Lord, you've let us see dry spells when we thought the
world would die for rain. I've known soul dryness like
that—and thought I could not live. Thank you, Lord, that
you sent your rain in time to our parched earth and that you
are, in us, rivers of living water, welling up to eternal life.

Multiplied by Love

Hallelujah, Lord, for your faithfulness to meet our every need.

Jesus shouted to the crowds, "If anyone is thirsty, let him come to me and drink. For the Scriptures declare that rivers of living water shall flow from the inmost being of anyone who believes in me."

—*John 7:37-38 TLB*

Follow Me

Visiting my child's class at the Central Institute for the Deaf in St. Louis, Missouri, I was part of the news for the day. The teacher had various children say it aloud: "'Guerite's mother came to school today," and then asked the whole class to go to the blackboard and write the sentence. 'Guerite, of course, was expected to write the same sentence, but using the pronoun *my* instead of her own name.

I watched as she went to the blackboard along with the rest of them. She wrote her *My* at once, then stopped to think for a moment. The word her chalk traced next was not *mother,* but *mama*—"My mama came to school today." As she passed my seat on the way back to her desk, she shot me a defiant glance.

"Not wrong, different," she explained with confident assurance, just in case I didn't know.

O Lord, how often the world judges a thing wrong just because it's different. Give me sense not to be that way. Let me judge the way my child does, who knows instinctively that something different may actually be better for her, closer to the truth of things. And keep me from an inordinate concern about what other people do. Give me grace to accept with thanksgiving the way you have planned for me and not to question what you have planned for another. Let me follow you.

Peter turned around and saw the disciple Jesus loved following . . . . Peter asked Jesus, "What about him, Lord? . . ." Jesus replied, ". . . What is that to you? You follow me."

—John 21:20-22 TLB

Be Beautiful Inside

I was breakfasting simply in a luxurious hotel restaurant. Ordering orange juice and scrambled eggs, coffee and toast, I enjoyed watching the crisply efficient waitresses as they walked about, writing orders on their neat little pads, setting tables with gleaming crystal and silver.

When my breakfast came, I was mystified. Perched atop my plate of toast was a peculiar looking blob of something shiny and a darkish orange in color. Gingerly moving it to one side, along with the contaminated piece of toast on which it rested so inelegantly and uncomfortably, I ate the rest of my breakfast. When the waitress came to refill my coffee cup, I pointed to the strange object still on my plate.

"What is that supposed to be?" I asked her. "A candied fig?" As I had studied the strange contours and complexion of the thing, that had seemed a plausible identity for it.

"No," she laughed, rather apologetically. "It's a small Danish pastry. They put it there to make the toast look better—I think," she went on.

Lord, I wonder how many of our attempts to beautify the beautiful (what is lovelier than a fresh plate of toast to one who is hungry for breakfast?) come out looking as unfortunate as that miserable blob on top of my toast? It probably added something to my bill, besides which, when I tasted it I found it quite inedible.

Lord, let that experience keep me from embellishing simple truth which is always better without any decoration. And Lord, plant your inner beauty of a gentle and quiet spirit in me.

Your beauty should not come from outward adornment. . . . Instead, it should be that of your inner self, the unfading beauty of a gentle and quiet spirit, which is of great worth in God's sight.

—I Peter 3:3-4 NIV

Know That
God Is Love

One night I was standing before a group of people, wondering what I was to say to them. I heard myself praying, "Lord, I don't know what they need to hear. I don't even know what I need to hear. But you know, Lord, and I ask you to provide the message for us out of your abundant supply." I went on to invite Him to take charge of that hour and do with it what He would out of His perfect will for our lives.

I suppose I had faith that He would use me to minister to them somehow, and so I launched out to share something God had been teaching me recently in experience and in His Word. As I spoke, I found myself beginning sentences whose endings I did not know until I heard them.

There was nothing so unusual about that. My husband and I had learned to trust Him for a message. Somehow that night I found myself quoting the scripture from I John 3:2 about how we don't know what we'll be like, but we do know this, that when He comes, we'll be like Him, because we will see Him as He really is. And it was given me to know and to share, as I stood there, the truth that what we'll be like when we're like Him is love, because He is love.

Multiplied by Love

Confessing before them—and Him—that love is mostly what I'm not, that my every failure is a failure to be love, I read confession in their faces too.

Just a few days before, He had given me a thought to scrawl large on a piece of paper and tape to my study wall:

> God sent His love
> and said
> Call His name Jesus
> All hail!

And it settles on me again, fresh and new and vital, just now as I write this, that *what it means to be like Jesus is to be love*.

Lord, help me die to self so you *can* be love through me. And, Lord, I thank you that even when we are so flooded with awareness of your love we think we will surely drown in it, we haven't even begun to taste it. Thank you that your love is eternal, without a bound of time, and infinite, without compass in its greatness. Thank you for your perfect illimitable love.

Keep yourselves in the love of God.

—*Jude 1:21*

Depend on the Lord

It was exciting to watch—the suspenseful drama of the squirrel coming down the pine tree to steal sunflower seeds from the bird feeder, the cat coming near, stalking the squirrel. The surreptitious movements of each as we held our breaths to see the outcome—

Suddenly, a huge barking dog bounded across the yard after a second cat that fairly flew up the pine, the first cat racing before him. The squirrel leaped from branch to interlacing branch and wound up in another tree on the far side of the yard.

As suddenly as the little drama had begun, the final curtain was drawn. And nobody came out for a curtain call that day.

Lord, do we too flirt with danger when we think our own cunning can outwit the enemy? Do we almost need something totally beyond us to teach us to fly to you, to realize that our only safety lies not in our cleverness or strength but in your loving and everlasting arms? If that's so, Lord, then let the unconquerable enemy come, that we might flee to you and know your peace and rest.

Multiplied by Love

The best-equipped army cannot save a king—for great strength is not enough to save anyone. A war horse is a poor risk for winning victories—it is strong but it cannot save. But the eyes of the Lord are watching over those who fear him, who rely upon his steady love. . . . We depend upon the Lord alone to save us.

—Psalm 33:16-20 TLB

Know the Lord

I had given our most grown-up son a new book to read, the true story of a man whose life was filled with miracles of God's love toward him. When Tommy finished reading the book, he handed it back to me.

"How did you like it?" I asked him.

"Great!" was his enthusiastic reply.

I questioned him further, probing a little.

"Do you mean to tell me you believe that God is still doing such things today?"

His reply exceeded all my expectations.

"Naw, Mama," he said, catching my gaze and holding it with the intensity in his voice, "I don't *believe* it—I *know* that it's true."

Hallelujah, Lord! How I thank you for imparting such faith to our son. Would that all young men and all the rest of us would come to such a certain knowledge of your reality and power. And thank you, Lord, that such knowledge, such certainty is available to us by your Holy Spirit and that your Holy Spirit is available to us for the asking. Thanks, Lord, for the wonderfulness of all that.

Multiplied by Love

I . . . ask the God of our Lord Jesus Christ, the glorious Father, to give you the Spirit, who will make you wise and reveal God to you, so that you will know him.
—Ephesians 1:17 TEV

"You know how to give good things to your children. How much more, then, the Father in heaven will give the Holy Spirit to those who ask him!"
—Luke 11:13 TEV

Put God in Charge

Once upon a time, when my husband or I received a telephone invitation to speak somewhere, we would tell the inviter that we would pray about the invitation and let him know our decision later. This wasn't convenient for anybody: the inviter usually needed a yes or no right away; we had better things to do with our time and money than to pay for long-distance phone calls or to write letters of acceptance or rejection.

Thinking about all this one day, we decided that we could spare ourselves and other people a great deal of inconvenience and expense if we prayed *before* we received an invitation instead of afterward. And so we began to change our standard operating procedure, praying something like this:

Lord, please take complete charge of our calendars. If you want us to go somewhere to speak, let someone invite us. If you don't want us to go, don't let us be invited, or if someone is so out of your will as to invite us anyway, put a conflict on our calendars so we'll have to refuse. In Jesus' name we ask it. Amen.

Well, the beforehand prayer worked out perfectly for quite a while. As we received invitations, we accepted or rejected them on the basis of our covenant with Him, and everywhere we went we were confident that the invitation had come from God Himself. It was good.

But then one day a letter came from a man in another state inviting us to come for a weekend of meetings. I'd always been thrilled at invitations before, but this one made me sputter inside. The nerve of that man, thinking we could travel such a distance to talk to his church!

I put the letter along with the rest of the day's mail on my husband's desk where he would see it when he came home from work. While I was preparing supper, he strode into the kitchen with the letter in his hand.

"Funny thing," he said. "You know I've always been glad to accept invitations before, but this one rubs me wrong somehow. I don't understand why, but I don't have the slightest desire to go to this man's church and talk—about anything."

When he had finished telling me his reaction, I shared with him my own, and we both wondered about it. Were we to write and tell the man we could not come? But there was no conflict on the calendar—

At bedtime, we prayed that God would have His way in it.

The next morning, Allen said he felt as if the Lord had told him, "Oh? So you don't want to go? Do you want to take your calendar out of my hand, then?"

"Oh, no, Lord," Allen was quick to protest. "We still want you to be in charge of it."

"Then you are willing to let our previous arrangement stand, to let me stay in charge and not take over the deciding yourself?"

"Oh, yes, Lord. Certainly." It was the only possible answer.

When we looked over our road maps together, a great and joyful desire welled up in both of us to accept the man's invitation. I sat down at my desk and typed out the most enthusiastic letter of acceptance I had ever written anyone.

A few weeks later, we received a brief reply. The man had been unable to staff the other parts of the planned retreat, and so he had been forced to cancel it for now. He said nothing about being in touch with us if things should work out later or anything like that. Just that he hoped he hadn't inconvenienced us.

Lord, I thank you that you are trustworthy to work all things out according to your perfect purpose for our lives. Lord, don't let us get in the way of your grace, ever. Keep on giving us the faith to trust you in everything. Keep on managing our calendars—and our lives. For we ask it in Jesus' name.

In all thy ways acknowledge him, and he shall direct thy paths.

—Proverbs 3:6

Give Thanks
for All Things

On a rainy morning a friend telephoned, discouraged and depressed over the slowness of her Christian growth.

"I feel so down, so far from God," she confessed. "Why, half the time, I even forget to thank God for our food when we sit down to eat. When you were a new Christian, did you ever forget to say grace at the table?"

"No," I answered, honestly and rather self-righteously. "Long before I ever knew what it really meant to be a Christian, saying grace at the table was a routine part of my life."

I didn't tell her just how awfully routine it had seemed to me during my growing-up years. The "grace" Papa said was always the same, and the words tumbled out so automatically, so rapidly that I couldn't understand them. To my child mind, they sounded like, "Father, griffus, gruffus, shoot the gun." In later years, I made out the very respectable words, "Father, forgive us our sins, and accept our thanks for this food and all thy blessings. Amen."

Good enough words, but I had never thought much about them.

Then, as my friend and I talked, sharing God's love over the telephone, an overwhelming thankfulness began to rise up in me for other routine things in life, everyday things that I never thought of saying "grace" over: a good night's rest; the soft rug under my feet when I stepped out of bed; a tub with warm water for my morning bath; fresh, clean clothes to put on; a stove to heat water for coffee, and bacon and eggs to put in the skillet; milk delivered to my doorstep and a refrigerator to keep it fresh; healthy, happy kids and a husband coming downstairs to breakfast; smiles on their faces; morning greetings full of love; eagerness for the day; school for the kids to go to, a job for my husband; satisfying work for me in the house; a cardinal in the dogwood tree outside my window; the telephone voice of my friend; the God who made it all—

Oh, I thought, how strange that I have righteously remembered to thank God routinely for food—three times a day or more—but haven't thought of giving thanks for and asking His blessing on all these other wonderful routine gifts of life. I wanted to start right then.

And suddenly I heard it, as if for the first time, the prayer Papa had prayed, thousands of times, "Father, forgive us our sins, and accept our thanks for this food *and all thy blessings.*" Why, all those years, in his three-times-a-day prayers, Papa had been giving thanks for everything!

Lord, I praise you for making my earthly father faithful to thank you for all our blessings. And today I thank you especially that you have brought me to the place where I know to thank you too.

At all times and for everything giving thanks in the name of our Lord Jesus Christ to God the Father.
—Ephesians 5:20 Amplified

Show the Fruit
of the Spirit

Marguerite was engrossed in the airport activity going on outside the airplane window beside her. A passenger stalled in the deboarding line watched her for a moment. "Does she like to fly?" he asked. He wasn't being fresh, just alive.

"Oh, she loves it. Heredity, I think," I grinned.

"Most kids do love it," he said, after a little pause.

He didn't look our way again until the line moved.

"Have a nice day," he called back to us, with a voice that would have made any day nice.

"God bless," I said to his back. He didn't turn, but I could see his cheek bulge in a secret smile, and I knew his pleasantness came from the Lord.

Lord, it is a precious thing to me that other people who really know you don't have to wear a man-made badge to be recognized. You make your joy visible in them. And how it blesses us to see it! Thank you, Lord, for the difference you make in our lives. Thank you that it shows.

By this shall all men know that ye are my disciples, if you have love one to another.

—John 13:35

Know That Death Is Swallowed Up in Victory

We seldom see victory where there's been no battle. I saw victory yesterday shining bright as the sun through pouring rain. The young widow sat, her children beside her, under the drab funeral tent in the clay-banked cemetery where the paths had turned to sticky glue in the downpour.

But it was hard to remember we were at a funeral and that the rain was pouring down. Because there was the joy of victory and peace in the eager smile of the young woman as she looked up to greet each one who shuffled by to extend sympathy, to wish her well.

There had been a battle, grueling and long, hard, but the cancer hadn't won in the end. The young man—what was really him—wasn't in the casket, and she knew it. "Gene has gone home," was how she put it. He was in glory—with the Lord—and in some mysterious way, the Lord was also with her, and so they were still together.

Lord, we cannot understand such grace as that. We can only receive it when such grace is what *we* need. How I praise you for your faithfulness, your limitless supplying of *all* we need. Thank you, Lord.

Multiplied by Love

Man goeth to his long home, . . . and the spirit shall return unto God who gave it.

—Ecclesiastes 12:5,7

He will swallow up death in victory; and the Lord God will wipe away tears from off all faces.

—Isaiah 25:8

Pray for Those Who Despitefully Use You

Marguerite had a tent, and she loved to go camping. One day, she and her little sister, Maria, pitched the tent on the school playground that adjoins our yard. They had a good time lugging sleeping bags, canteens, pillows, and blankets to furnish it for their play. That night, they came home to bed and left the tent with all its paraphernalia on the playground. The next morning, it was gone. There was no trace of any of it—except the holes where the tent stakes had been.

We wondered why God had allowed this thing to happen. Was it that the kids might learn responsibility in taking care of their things? Or that I might teach it better than I had up to that time? After a while, we decided that neither of those things was what it was all about. The thing had happened that we might pray for the thieves.

That day, I saw that in everything that happens, God is working to reconcile the world to Himself. It's made me newly thankful—even for lost tents and the disappearance of the last decent pillows in the house.

The kids got a new tent, eventually. And I never had to

remind them not to leave it on the playground. But I didn't learn the best lesson of all from the episode until some weeks later when I was reading the Bible. "Pray for them which despitefully use you," Jesus said. "Well, we have done that," I assured myself, and read on.

After a few more instructions about how we are to treat other people, Jesus tells us that our reward for doing these things shall be great.

I had always supposed that the great reward for such things as praying for those who despitefully use us would be something in the nature of a pat on the head when we reached heaven, and His voice saying, "Well done, good and faithful servant," but suddenly, the verse was illuminated with an exciting new revelation:

Our praying for those who despitefully use us is not just to make us feel better about it and avoid the ulcers and arthritis of unforgiveness and resentment. Our prayers are the very means He has designed for bringing the offenders into the Kingdom!

When we get to heaven, we will see the offenders there, the ones for whom we have prayed, all shiny with the newness of sins forgiven. They will be saved because we have followed Jesus' instructions to pray for them. He will have heard and honored the prayers!

Wow, Lord, wow! Talk about a great reward—that one will take the cake. Think of it! We hold the power of eternal life and death in our hands for those who misuse us in this life! We can hold a grudge and condemn them and ourselves to something less than abundant life in the here and now, or we can pray for them and have a fantastically joyful reunion in heaven.

I like being part of that, Lord. Thanks for giving us such a neat plan to follow. And now plant nothing less than your forgiving love in us that we will be able to follow through.

Lord, I thank you for the whomsoevers who stole the tent. Please lead them to somebody who will introduce them to you. I ask it in Jesus' name.

Love ye your enemies, and do good, and lend, hoping for nothing again; and your reward shall be great, and ye shall be the children of the Highest.

—Luke 6:35

Come unto Me

Crucifixion

Dogwood branches:
arms outstretched
white crosses beckoning
Come unto me

Lord, some days I see it, all nature proclaiming your love—ocean waves thundering it, cirrus clouds whispering it, with untold voices filling the whole range between. O Lord, let me see your infinite love every day and share it with power. In Jesus' name.

Ever since God created the world, his invisible qualities, both his eternal power and his divine nature, have been clearly seen. Men can perceive them in the things that God has made.

—Romans 1:20 TEV

Come unto me, all ye that labour and are heavy laden, and I will give you rest.

—Matthew 11:28

Avoid Godless Racket

Some kids wonder, sometimes, why I don't like the raucous rock music from the juke box at the current drive-in hangout for the high school crowd. The answer is simple: I don't feel God in it. (Does anyone?) I'm so deaf to Him in it that I can't imagine how anyone would prefer listening to it instead of to silence. That it destroys the hearing of those who listen is surely God's mercy to them, dimming the world outside so they can hear Him who speaks within.

Lord, let my soul be still and know that you are God!

But shun profane and vain babblings: for they will increase unto more ungodliness.

—II Timothy 2:16

Love, Love, Love

My very first plane ride happened more than twenty years ago. It was a memorable one: I was too excited, the flight being for the purpose of going from my Ohio home to North Carolina to visit a young law student I hadn't seen for two years. The weather was gusty, and I didn't know *not* to sit in the tail of the smallish plane.

I fastened my seat belt carefully, hoping it wouldn't wrinkle my skirt (we were not permanent pressed in those days). But all impressions of takeoff and climbing and looking below were almost immediately erased by an awareness of people hovering over me, patting my arms, putting an oxygen mask over my face, wrapping me in a blanket, bringing me a pill to take as I watched, helplessly entranced, while my hand slowly crushed the paper cup of water a flight attendant had handed me. I think a doctor aboard called my trouble "hyperventilation," but it may have been just the opposite. I was breathless, all right. Must have fainted.

At our first stop, some man took me outside and walked me up and down in drizzling rain on the concrete runway of a middle-of-nowhere airport.

Love, Love, Love

"You ought to get a cab to the bus station and head for home, miss," he said to me, sympathizing. I considered it briefly, looking down at what had been a crisp new suit, now thoroughly rumpled and bedraggled, and knowing that the rain had ruined the curl in my hair.

"No thanks," I said, deciding against it, and then going on with shaky confidence, "I think I'll be all right." In those days, I always carried out *my* intentions, no matter what.

That flight thoroughly initiated me into a brand-new world of air travel, and I had interesting answers for the earnest young man who met me at the airport and asked, "Did you have a good flight?"

He didn't seem to mind my disheveled attire. We were married the following year, and as I write this recollection, we're past our twenty-third anniversary, six kids later.

Ever since that first unforgettable trip, I've loved flying and have had occasion to fly with increasing frequency in the last few years. It still thrills me to feel the thrust of power shoving me back in my seat as a big jet is airborne, to see the things of earth get smaller and smaller as the plane climbs higher and higher. Watching the ever-changing tapestry of earth below, I like to think that God gives me a hint of His perspective on things.

In the air above Chicago one day, I was overwhelmed by the number of dwelling places I could see out my window. I thought of all the people who must live in the houses—so many! Was it possible that God could be looking down with love on everyone in every house, that He could be as intimately involved in their lives as I felt Him to be in mine?

The question "blew my mind," and I shoved it aside and

turned the page of the devotional book I had been reading.

The answer to my question was perfect in the poem that greeted my eyes on the printed page:

> Among so many, can He care?
> Can special love be everywhere?
> A myriad homes,—a myriad ways,—
> And God's eye over every place?
>
> I asked: my soul bethought of this;—
> In just that very place of His
> Where He hath put and keepeth you,
> God hath no other thing to do!
>
> —Adeline D. T. Whitney

It was more than enough to stagger the imagination. I decided to try a little experiment in seeing as God sees when the plane landed. As passengers filed by me to leave the plane and as more passengers got on to search for seats, I looked at each one, imagining that he was my brother, sister, mother, father, son or daughter, or a friend dear to me. When we were airborne again, I tried looking down on the houses as if each one was occupied by someone very special to me. What joy welled in me as I imagined that house was where our son Tommy lived, that one where my parents stayed! What love I felt!

And in the welling up, I saw it. *It is so!* Each stranger, each occupant of each house is *supposed* to be that dear to me, because I am commanded to love as He loves.

Lord, I know that in my humanness, I'll never make it—I'll never be able to love as You love—but thanks for giving me, that day, a glimpse into your heart. And hasten the day when we will see you so clearly that we will be like you.

> *I give you a new commandment:*
> *love one another;*
> *just as I have loved you,*
> *you also must love one another.*
> *—John 13:34 JB*

In Everything
Give Thanks

Fierce April gusts buffeted the plane and blew the air full of dust from the freshly plowed farmland near the airport. Waiting for takeoff, I heard the click of the intercom and then the pilot's voice telling us that we would be going to 10,000 feet for the continuation of our jet flight to Washington National Airport.

"It will be a little bumpy going up," he informed us, "kind of bumpy along the way, and bumpy going down because of the wind." Having said that without apology, just as a statement of fact, the pilot added a crisp "Thank you," and the intercom fell silent.

Why did he say thank you? I asked myself as we were thrust back in our seats by the steep angle of the climb. Thanks for listening? Or thanks for not blaming me for the weather? Or maybe, I mused, the pilot was being thankful for the wind that kept any lack of smoothness in the flight from being his fault.

Whatever the source of the pilot's thank you—and it could have been mere routine or a requirement that he sign off with those words—I found myself suddenly brimming with thanksgiving of my own. There were a number of things *worth* being thankful for: the clear day for flying; that God had moved obstacle mountains to make it possible for my husband to accompany me on the weekend trip; that there was no fear in me when the plane lurched suddenly to the right, then bounced back abruptly in the other direction; that the sudden plunging of my innards was an interesting observation, not a thing of terror.

But as I meditated, I realized that my immense thanksgiving was not from any one of those things, nor from the whole collection of them. My thanksgiving was overflowing from the certain knowledge that God Himself is in charge of my life, and that He loves me so much—in life or in death—that nothing else matters besides. That's a good thing to know—on a windy day in an airplane or on a still day at home.

Lord, thank you, thank you, thank you.

In every thing give thanks: for this is the will of God in Christ Jesus concerning you.

—I Thessalonians 5:18

Know That with God All Things Are Possible

A woman telephoned me one morning from a town forty miles away. She was deeply concerned about a twenty-year-old girl who was fed up with a life of alcohol, cigarettes, pot, drugs of all kinds, *and* homosexuality.

"May I bring her to see you and your husband?" she asked.

Everything inside me screamed "No!" Out loud, I recommended several ministers in her area who would be equipped to cope with such sordidness as she had told me about.

"I've already tried to contact all of them," she said," but no one was available. The girl is desperate for help *now.*"

Still trying to get out of being involved, I encouraged the woman to continue to pray and to depend on Jesus to heal her friend, but she wouldn't let me cop out.

"All right," I finally agreed. "You may bring her at eight o'clock tonight."

Promptly at eight, the front doorbell rang, and in came the woman who had called me, her husband, a Spirit-filled Christian friend, and the girl. Within a few minutes, the three all-right persons left—to go shopping for a while, they said—and we turned our attention to the girl who was slumped in the corner of the couch. She wore tight blue jeans, a boy's jacket, had close-cropped dark hair, and the deadest looking eyes I'd ever seen. Her face was expressionless as she poured out her story while my husband and I listened.

She had grown up in a religious home, she said, been a church member most of her life, a leader in the youth organization, one of the counselors up front at revival meetings to lead other people to Jesus. Her church didn't ignore the gifts of the Holy Spirit; it preached against them, said they were for Bible times, not for today. When she was in the ninth grade, she had played with a Ouija board—"harmless, just a game," she said—and the young girl who had worked the Ouija board with her became the first of her sex partners in perversion.

As I listened, I wept, praying under my breath, thanking Jesus for His love and praising Him that He is powerful to deliver from the very depths of hell. Hell seemed to be where she was.

"I'm ready to split," she said. "To go somewhere, just anywhere. My life is used up."

Depressed, my mind was tempted to analyze her neatly, *a good candidate for psychiatry.* But she had been to five psychiatrists in the last three years. All of them had tried to help her by encouraging her to know herself, and the more she knew herself, the more she hated the stench of her life.

"But I can't change," she said, in the same dull monotone in which she had told the rest of her story. "And, besides, I'm not sure that I want to change. Only there's no peace in my life anymore."

She stopped talking, just sat there, her dull eyes staring at nothing. My husband began to talk to her, using scriptures that had always been effective in dealing with other people, but there was no budging her with Scripture. She could quote it almost better than he could. And, she assured him, she'd been ministered to by many other people, and it hadn't done any good.

I kept talking softly to the Lord, mostly in a language I had never learned, because *perfect* prayer was needed, not prayer that might be fouled up by my thinking or asking amiss. Tears kept washing down my face, and I knew the copious flow was not mine, it was the overflowing of the Holy Spirit. Jesus said that rivers of living water would well up in anyone who believed, and living water has to flow somewhere. I was believing Him, trusting Him, all right, because there was no help aside from Him and we knew it.

Finally, the Word began to get through, and the girl agreed to pray the sinner's prayer, confessing her sins, asking God to forgive her, and thanking Him for His forgiveness. Then Allen led her in a prayer asking for the infilling of the Holy Spirit that she might be empowered to live the life of new creaturehood that Jesus had promised to all who receive Him. Afterward, she looked a *little* brighter, said she felt somewhat better.

About that time, the girl's friends returned to take her home—not to stay, just for the night—so she could get her things. We were to take her to Raleigh the next day, to see if there might be a place for her to live in the Christian community at Nicky Cruz Girls' Home for a while. There, in a sheltered, disciplined environment, she could learn to walk in her new life and be strengthened in it without being tempted by old associations.

Know That with God All Things Are Possible

I was grateful there was such a place to take her. But the next day, when we arrived at the Home, we learned that Nicky was out of town and that in the case of this particular girl, he would have to interview her and make the decision as to whether or not she could be taken in. Among the residents of the Home were former topless dancers and prostitutes—who could present a difficult temptation for one with this girl's problem. She was still a lesbian, still hooked on drugs, still craving cigarettes. Sometimes, they told us, the nicotine habit is one of the hardest of all to break.

"Take her home with you, and bring her back tomorrow," we were told. "Nicky can see her and make the decision then."

Oh, no! I didn't want to take another day away from my work. Besides, I didn't like the thought of having her spend the night at our house—not with little children, teen-age daughters and sons there. Racking my brain to get out of it, I came up with the perfect solution: I would call a devout Christian woman who had a prayer group in her Raleigh home and ask her to take the girl in just for the night. I wouldn't have to tell her much about the girl, and I could go back home to business as usual.

But the woman turned me down cold, and I saw there was no choice; we would have to take the girl back home with us. God wasn't finished with our part of it.

The staff of the Home prayed with us—I prayed most fervently of all—that God would protect us all from harm, and we headed for home. On the way, the girl told me that she didn't sleep much, and I knew I wouldn't sleep at all with her in the house. Why, she might accidentally set fire

107

to it, she might run away, she might— My imagination roared full steam ahead.

After supper at a restaurant, where she was in agony because we asked her not to smoke, my husband took the girl and one of our daughters to an evening service at a charismatic church, a church whose fellowship believes that the gifts of the Holy Spirit—all of them—*are* for today. I stayed home to put our little girl to bed, to work, to pray, and to dread what the night might bring.

It was late when they came home, and almost without looking up, I handed the girl a couple of pages to read from a new manuscript on my desk. I thought the article might help her with her smoking habit. She sat down in a chair beside my desk to read, then handed the pages back to me after a minute, *grinning!*

Something was wrong! The piece was supposed to make the reader cry! Seeing the bewilderment on my face, the girl laughed.

"Oh, don't misunderstand," she said. "The article is just great. But I didn't need to read it. I've been delivered!"

And then I really looked at her. There was a change all right. It was obvious that new creaturehood had set in. For a couple of hours the three of us sat up and shared the powerful love of Jesus together.

The girl told me how the pastor and one of the women in the congregation had taken her aside for special ministry, and how as they prayed, she had reached into her jacket pocket and taken out her cigarettes. "I knew I wouldn't need them anymore," she said. She told me too how she had felt all the old cravings and perverted desires just draining out of her. She knew she had been cleansed, really cleansed by the blood of Jesus. The work that had been begun in her the day before was going on to completion.

Finally, we all went to bed, rejoicing, full of blessing.

But the next morning, the kids got up and off to school, I got dressed for the day, Allen left for court, and there was still no sound from the room upstairs at the end of the hall. I left a place set at the table, and the leftover bacon and eggs and grits congealed in their pans on the stove.

My imagination began roaring again. The thought I wanted to make *stick* was the joyful one, "He giveth to his beloved in sleep," but other thoughts kept crowding it out, thoughts like, "Maybe her deliverance didn't last. Maybe she died from an overdose of something. Maybe she decided living up to a new life would be too hard and she ran away. Maybe—"

But at ten o'clock, there began to be alive noises upstairs. I could hear the shower running.

After a bit, she came downstairs— The dead girl was completely gone, and in her place was one of the prettiest, most alive *girls* I'd ever seen. Her skin had a new glow. The boyishness of her clothes only served to accentuate her femininity. She had slept so soundly she hadn't even heard our noisy household getting off for the day. It was the first night in years that she had gone to bed without drinking beer and "doing dope." And, she told me, before she had gone to sleep, she had suddenly, surprisingly, found herself praising Jesus in a language she had never learned. And she felt *such power*. She had to keep pinching herself to see if it was real.

The newness in her was so tangible, I took her to see a local minister that morning. The impromptu testimony she gave him left nothing out. She told him all about herself, about her good friend who had killed himself, about her dead church, about what all the kids she knew were looking for and how they had turned to supernatural Satanic power when they didn't see any other power at work. She was so anointed, I listened enthralled, and the minister did too. It was one of the most exciting half hours of my life.

After lunch, on the way to Raleigh again, the girl laughed out loud and explained that smokers always *have* to have a cigarette after eating. "But I don't even *want* one!" she laughed, still rejoicing.

When we walked into the Home, the director—a vibrant Catholic nun—took one look at her and exclaimed, "Why, why, that's a *new girl!*" Nicky talked to her, straight and hard, prayed with her, had her pray herself and read the fifth chapter of Ephesians aloud to him. Then he hugged her hard enough to break every rib in her body, and she hugged him back. There was no question about her not being permitted to stay at the Home now that her problem was a thing of the past.

The girl stayed at the Home, witnessing to women in prison, attending Nicky's crusades with the other girls, giving her testimony in churches until she had her feet firmly on the ground in a wholesome new life-style. The last I heard, she had a good job and was planning to enroll in a Christian university the coming fall.

Oh, yes. The girl's name is Angela, Angie for short. It didn't fit before; it does now. Sometimes God changes our name when He makes us into new creatures. Sometimes He lets us begin to fit the name He had given us already.

Know That with God All Things Are Possible

O Lord, how I thank you and praise you that you sent the desperate young girl to us. How I thank you that you didn't want us to do something for her, but that you were planning to do something for her yourself and loved us enough to give us front-row seats for the most exciting drama of the year. How I praise you for imparting your empowering Holy Spirit to your church, that it might do the very things that Jesus did when he was here on earth—and greater things because He has gone to the Father.

Lord, all this is too marvelous for me. I thank you, Lord, for delivering Angela from all her afflictions, for saving her from a death-life of sin and for giving her everlasting life in you. How I thank you for changing her almost in the twinkling of an eye from some*thing* so ugly to some*one* so beautiful.

Lord, we have friends who tell us that the *full* gospel, Holy Spirit baptism, and the gifts of the Holy Spirit are not for them. And yet they want to help people. Some of them claim they are called to a ministry of love or social action. That they are just going to help people by loving them with their own human love.

Lord, I weep over such limited ministries. What could the most dedicated, noble, human love have done for Angie? The most sophisticated modern psychiatry? If that's all there had been to help her in her hour of need, she'd be no longer in her old life of sin, she'd be in the grave.

But, Lord, pardon me for telling you all this. It's you who know it already, and you who have shown us so clearly that it is so. O Lord, how you must yearn to reach all your people with the powerful message of the fullness of your redeeming, life-changing love that no one may be left out of it.

Father, I thank you that you forever use such earthen vessels as we are to hold the priceless treasure that you are. Give the world to see you and not the vessel at all, to hear you and not the vessel at all. And so let them be blessed. I ask it, fervently, in Jesus' holy wonderful name.

Jesus answered them, "Truly, truly, I say to you, every one who commits sin is the slave of sin. . . . You shall know the truth, and the truth shall make you free. . . . If therefore the Son shall make you free, you shall be free indeed."

—John 8:34, 32, 36 NAS